Worlds of Wisdom™

FISHING

The Art of Living, One Insight at a Time

LUSTER

Asher Erskine

What is Worlds of Wisdom?

Wisdom is everywhere – woven into every craft, discipline, and tradition.
Some lessons are learned through practice, others are passed down
through generations, standing the test of time. Often, the most powerful
insights come from unexpected places, revealing surprising connections
between seemingly unrelated fields.

Worlds of Wisdom brings these timeless teachings together into one
beautifully curated series – designed to be both a source of inspiration
and a guide for action. Whether exploring familiar ideas or uncovering
new perspectives, each volume offers a lens through which to see the
world differently.

Step into the *Worlds of Wisdom* and discover *The Art of Living, One Insight
at a Time*.

Introduction to Fishing

Fishing is one of the oldest activities practiced by humans, dating back to ancient times. Whether for survival, sport, or recreation, it has evolved into a multi-billion-dollar industry worldwide. Fishing is about more than just catching fish – it's a connection to nature, patience, and skill. It's an art form for some, a livelihood for others, and a peaceful pastime for millions of enthusiasts.

Fishing involves the pursuit of aquatic creatures, particularly fish, using various techniques and tools such as rods, reels, nets, and spears. Types of fishing range from freshwater fishing in rivers and lakes to saltwater fishing in oceans and seas, each offering unique challenges and rewards. The sport continues to adapt with technology, from eco-friendly fishing practices to innovations in gear.

History

Fishing has been a vital practice throughout human history. The earliest evidence of fishing dates back over 40,000 years to ancient cave paintings and artefacts discovered in locations like Spain and France. Early civilisations like the Egyptians, Greeks, and Romans relied heavily on fishing for food, and the methods they developed continue to influence modern practices.

The development of fishing tools, such as spears and hooks made from bone, led to more efficient methods of catching fish. By the Middle Ages, fishing became a staple of European diets, especially in regions near large bodies of water. The invention of the fishing reel in the 17th century revolutionised the practice, making it more accessible and efficient. Over time, recreational fishing emerged as a leisure activity, particularly in the 19th and 20th centuries, leading to the growth of clubs, competitions, and organised events.

Today, fishing continues to evolve, with a focus on sustainability and conservation. Modern fishing techniques, such as fly fishing, deep-sea fishing, and catch-and-release, demonstrate how far the practice has come while striving to preserve aquatic ecosystems for future generations.

Gear

The right fishing gear is essential to a successful fishing experience. Fishing gear has evolved over time, with new materials, designs, and innovations improving the effectiveness and comfort of anglers. Here's an overview of the core fishing gear every angler should know about:

Fishing Rods

The fishing rod is one of the most crucial pieces of equipment. There are different types of rods designed for specific fishing techniques, including spinning rods, casting rods, fly rods, and trolling rods. The length, material, and action (how the rod bends) all influence the rod's performance. For example, a longer rod can cast further, while a stiffer rod provides more control over larger fish.

Fishing Reels

A fishing reel is mounted on the rod and is used to wind in the fishing line after a catch. There are several types of reels: spinning reels, bait-casting reels, and fly reels. Each reel type is suited to a specific style of fishing. Spinning reels are commonly used for light to medium fishing, while bait-casting reels are preferred for larger fish due to their increased precision and power.

Fishing Lines

Fishing lines come in various materials, including monofilament, fluorocarbon, and braided lines. Monofilament is the most common and versatile, ideal for a variety of fishing techniques. Fluorocarbon is nearly invisible underwater, making it a great choice for wary fish, while braided lines offer strength and durability for larger fish.

Hooks and Lures

Hooks are essential for catching fish, and they come in various sizes and designs, depending on the species and fishing method. Lures mimic the movements and appearance of prey, attracting fish to bite. Common lures include spinners, jigs, and soft plastics. Live bait such as worms or minnows can also be used to increase the chances of catching fish.

Bait and Chum

Bait can be live (e.g., worms, minnows, or insects), dead (e.g., cut-up fish or shrimp), or artificial (e.g., lures). Some anglers also use chum, a mixture of ground fish or other attractants, to create a scent trail that draws fish closer to the fishing area. The choice of bait depends on the fish species you're targeting and the water conditions.

Tackle Boxes and Bags

A tackle box or bag is used to organise and store fishing gear such as hooks, lures, lines, and other accessories. A well-organised tackle box makes it easier to quickly access the necessary gear while fishing.

Fishing Nets

Nets are essential for landing fish, especially larger ones. There are many types of nets, from small landing nets used for smaller fish to larger fish-handling nets used for big game species. Some nets are designed for catch-and-release, with soft mesh to avoid harming the fish.

Fishing Clothing and Accessories

Proper clothing can make a huge difference in your comfort while fishing. This includes items such as waterproof jackets, waders for fishing in rivers or lakes, hats, and polarised sunglasses to reduce glare on the water. Some anglers also use gloves, sun protection, and fishing tools like pliers, fish grippers, and scales to make handling fish easier and safer.

Fishing Styles and Techniques

Fishing has developed a wide range of styles and techniques, each offering its own challenges and rewards. The type of fishing you choose can depend on your location, the species of fish you're targeting, and personal preferences. Here are

some of the most popular fishing
styles and techniques:

Fly Fishing

Fly fishing is an angling technique
that uses an artificial fly – usually
made from feathers, fur, or other
materials – cast onto the water using
a specialised lightweight rod and reel.
This technique is typically associated
with catching trout, salmon, and
other freshwater fish, often in serene
environments. Fly fishing is renowned
for its precision and the skill it takes
to master the delicate art of casting.

Trolling

Trolling is a technique used mostly in
saltwater fishing where anglers drag
baited lines behind a moving boat. It's
ideal for targeting species like marlin,
tuna, and walleye, as it covers a large
area of water and can attract fish from
great distances. Trolling is often used
in both recreational and competitive
fishing, and is one of the best ways
to catch large fish.

Ice Fishing

Ice fishing is a winter activity that
involves fishing through a hole cut
into the ice on a frozen body of water.
It can be done using a simple hand-
held line or more elaborate ice-fishing
gear. Common fish targeted in ice
fishing include perch, pike, and trout.
The technique requires patience, as
anglers must wait for bites in often
harsh conditions.

Shore Fishing

Shore fishing, or bank fishing,
involves fishing from the shoreline of
a lake, river, or ocean. It's one of the
most accessible methods, requiring
minimal equipment. Common targets
include bass, carp, and other species
that inhabit shallow waters close to
shore. Shore fishing offers a relaxed
and flexible approach for both
beginners and experienced anglers.

Deep-Sea Fishing

Also known as offshore fishing,
deep-sea fishing takes place far from
shore, targeting large, powerful fish
species like marlin, swordfish, and
sharks. Anglers use heavy-duty
equipment to withstand the intense
forces of these fish. This technique
can involve bottom fishing, where the
bait is placed near the ocean floor,
or pelagic fishing, where the bait is
presented in the upper water column.

Catch and Release

Catch and release is a practice used
to minimise the impact of fishing on
fish populations and ecosystems.
After catching a fish, anglers carefully
return it to the water without keeping
it for food. This practice is common
across many types of fishing and is
especially important for protecting
endangered species and promoting
sustainable fisheries.

Herbert Hoover

"To go fishing is the chance to wash one's soul with pure air."

Fishing can affect our very core. The open air, the soothing rhythm of the water, and the quiet patience it requires create a rare opportunity to reset. In these moments, we reconnect with a sense of simplicity that so often gets lost in the rush of daily life.

"No man ever steps in the same river twice, for it's not the same river and he's not the same man."

Every experience leaves its mark, changing both the person and the world around them. The man and the river are forever altered by their encounter – a bond that reminds us how life is a constant flow of transformation.

"If people concentrated on the really important things in life, there'd be a shortage of fishing poles."

True priorities aren't dictated by trends or others' opinions but by the joy and meaning they bring. Fishing reminds us to focus on what feels essential, even if it seems simple or trivial to others.

"A ship in harbour is safe, but that is not what ships are built for."

Comfort zones may feel secure, but life's purpose lies beyond them. Ships are designed to face the sea, just as we are built to embrace challenges, fulfil our potential, and grow through meaningful risks.

"When fishermen cannot go to sea, they repair nets."

Temporary setbacks don't mean progress has to stop. Use quiet moments to prepare, refine your tools, and stay ready for opportunities. Success is built not only on big leaps but on steady, purposeful preparation.

"The sea, once it casts its spell, holds one in its net of wonder forever."

The sea is a place of endless fascination – vast, mysterious, and full of beauty. Once you've experienced its power, it lingers long after, offering lessons of humility, awe, and the infinite potential of the world around us.

"Many men go fishing all their lives without knowing that it is not fish they are after."

The act of fishing is often a quest for something far deeper than fish. It might be a longing for peace, a desire to reconnect with nature, or simply an excuse to escape life's noise. Fishing reminds us to look beyond the surface and recognise what truly matters to us.

"It's called fishing, not catching."

Fishing is a lesson in patience and presence. It reminds us that the act itself is enough – that we don't need results to justify the effort. Joy comes from being in the moment, embracing the process, and finding value in simply doing.

"Fishing is not an escape from life, but often a deeper immersion into it."

Far from an escape, fishing is a way to dive deeper into the present moment. It brings focus, calm, and clarity, offering an opportunity to immerse yourself in life's rhythms. It's an act of connection – both to the natural world and to yourself.

"The cure for anything is salt water: sweat, tears, or the sea."

Whether it's the hard work of sweat, the emotional release of tears, or the healing embrace of the sea, salt water has a way of renewing us. It speaks to the resilience of the human spirit and the power of life's most natural elements to restore balance.

"The river has great wisdom and whispers its secrets to the hearts of men."

The natural world offers many lessons, but they aren't shouted – they're whispered. It takes patience, openness, and attentiveness to understand its wisdom. For those willing to listen, nature offers truths that speak directly to the soul.

Carl Safina

"Fishing provides time to think, and reason not to."

Fishing creates a rare balance: a space for deep thought and the absence of it. Whether you reflect inwards or simply let your mind rest, it provides a sense of peace and clarity, making room for whatever you need most in the moment.

"Fishermen know that the sea is dangerous and the storm terrible, but they have never found these dangers sufficient reason to remain ashore."

The greatest achievements come with great risks. Fishermen face the perils of the sea because they know the rewards are worth it. It's a reminder that courage, perseverance, and the willingness to face challenges are essential to a meaningful life.

"If we save the sea, we save our world."

The health of the sea reflects the health of our world. Preserving it is crucial for the balance of all life on Earth.

Robert Traver

"The best time to go fishing is when you can get away."

In the busyness of life, it's easy to put off moments of peace. But just as fishing entices us to step away, so too does life. Taking time to disconnect, even briefly, refreshes the mind and restores balance.

"The beauty of fishing is that it's a different experience every time you do it."

Fishing, like life, is never the same twice. Each cast offers a new chance to learn, grow, and discover something unexpected. It reminds us that even in repetition, there's always room for fresh experiences and insights.

"Some go to church and think about fishing, others go fishing and think about God."

Fishing has a unique way of bringing clarity and perspective. For some, it's a quiet space for spiritual reflection, a moment to connect with something greater than themselves. It's a reminder that peace can be found in nature, where thoughts and spirit can align.

"A river cuts through rock, not because of its power, but because of its persistence."

Great achievements aren't always the result of sheer strength, but of consistent effort. Just as a river wears down rock over time, persistence – no matter how slow or quiet – can overcome the toughest obstacles. Patience and determination are often more powerful than force.

"The sea, the great unifier, is man's only hope. Now, as never before, the old phrase has a literal meaning: we are all in the same boat."

The sea reminds us of our shared humanity. In the vastness of the ocean, we are all equal, facing the same challenges. It's a call to recognise our interdependence and work together, for we all share this world and must navigate its waters as one.

"In a calm sea, every man is a pilot."

When conditions are easy, anyone can feel in control. But true skill is shown when the waters are rough. Life's challenges test our abilities, pushing us to grow and adapt. Calm times are a chance to prepare, but it's in the storm that we discover what we're truly capable of.

"Water is the driving force of all nature."

Water is the lifeblood of the Earth, shaping landscapes, sustaining life, and moving through every part of nature. It reminds us that flow and adaptability are essential forces in life. Just as water finds its path through obstacles, we too can navigate challenges with persistence and flexibility.

"An angler must be a student not only of fish but of lakes, rivers, and the air above them."

Fishing teaches us to observe and understand the world in its entirety. It's not just about catching fish but about recognising the interconnectedness of nature. The more we pay attention to the environment – its rhythms, patterns, and changes – the more we can navigate life with wisdom and awareness.

Joseph Conrad

"The sea has never been friendly to man. At most it has been the accomplice of human restlessness."

The unpredictable and vast sea reflects our own inner turmoil and yearning for exploration. It's not a gentle partner but a challenging force that mirrors our restlessness. Yet, it's in this challenge that we find growth – pushing beyond our comfort zones to discover something greater.

"A river is water in its loveliest form; rivers have life and sound and movement and infinity of variation, rivers are veins of the earth through which the lifeblood returns to the heart."

Rivers are more than just waterways; they are the lifeblood of the land, shaping everything in their path. Just as blood sustains the body, rivers bring vitality to the world around them, showing us the power of movement and transformation in nurturing growth and change.

"We forget that the water cycle and the life cycle are one."

Water is the thread that connects all life, constantly moving, renewing, and sustaining. Just as water flows through the Earth, so does life – an ongoing cycle of renewal and change. We often overlook this harmony, but it reminds us that every part of nature is deeply intertwined, and our existence depends on the balance of both.

"The river has taught me to listen; you will learn the same if you sit by its banks."

The river speaks not through words, but through its gentle flow, its quiet rhythm. By simply being present, we learn to listen – to the world around us, to the silence, and to ourselves. It teaches patience and presence, showing that wisdom often comes not from seeking answers, but from taking the time to truly hear.

"To fish is to live in harmony with time, with nature, and with oneself."

Fishing brings us into balance with the world around us. Its slow, steady rhythm clears the noise from our minds and roots us in something timeless – a quiet reminder of who we are beneath the rush of life.

"The fisherman knows the art of patience and the poetry of stillness."

Fishing teaches us that patience is not just waiting – it's an active, mindful state. In the stillness, there's a quiet beauty, a deeper awareness that can't be rushed. The fisherman understands that some of life's greatest rewards come in the spaces between action.

"The great charm of fly-fishing is that we are always learning."

Fly-fishing is a constant journey of discovery. Each cast, each shift in the current, teaches us something new – about the water, the fish, and ourselves. It reminds us that growth comes from embracing the process, and that mastery is built through patience and continuous learning.

"Fishing, the art of thinking while you are doing something."

Fishing is more than just an activity; it's a space where thoughts flow as freely as the water. It's the art of reflection, where the mind wanders and focuses at once. In this balance, we find clarity, quieting the noise and allowing our thoughts to unfold naturally.

"I have fished through fishless days that I remember happily without regret."

Fishing isn't just about the catch; it's about the experience. Even on days when the fish don't bite, there's joy in the quiet moments, in the act itself. It's a reminder that sometimes, the value of an experience isn't in the outcome, but in the peace we find along the way.

"Even a fish wouldn't get into trouble if it kept its mouth shut."

Silence is often a wiser choice than speaking out of turn. Just as a fish avoids danger by staying quiet, we too can avoid unnecessary conflict by choosing when to speak and when to listen. Sometimes, stillness brings clarity and protection.

"The wise fisherman knows that satisfaction is not always measured in the size of the catch."

True fulfilment in fishing – and in life – isn't about the results, but the experience. The wisdom of the fisherman lies in appreciating the process, the connection to nature, and the peace found in the moment, regardless of the outcome.

"Fishing provides that connection with the whole living world. It gives you the opportunity of being totally immersed, turning back into yourself in a good way."

Fishing offers more than just time spent by the water; it's an invitation to reconnect with life in its purest form. In the quiet immersion of nature, we find space to reflect, to return to ourselves, and to experience a deeper sense of belonging and peace.

"The fishing is good in troubled waters."

Sometimes, it's in moments of chaos or uncertainty that we find the greatest opportunities. Just as fish thrive in murky waters, challenges often present hidden chances for growth, learning, and success – if we're willing to look beneath the surface.

Izaak Walton

"Angling may be said to be so like the mathematics that it can never be fully learned."

Fishing, like mathematics, is a constant exploration of patterns, variables, and possibilities. It's an art of precision and patience, where mastery is always just beyond reach, inviting us to keep learning, improving, and embracing the process of discovery.

"Most of the world is covered by water. A fisherman's job is simple: Pick out the best parts."

Fishing teaches us to seek out the moments that matter. With the vastness of the world around us, it's about finding those rare, beautiful pockets of time and space – the ones that resonate deeply and offer true meaning, just like finding the perfect spot on the water.

"Those who fish get to know and understand a river in a way few others can."

Fishing invites us to witness the river's subtle rhythms – its flow, its quiet changes, and its hidden patterns. Those who fish become attuned to its language, gaining a deeper understanding of its mysteries and the life it supports, in a way that others may never see.

"The best fishermen
I know try not to make
the same mistakes over
and over again; instead,
they strive to make new
and interesting mistakes
and to remember what
they learned from them."

The journey of fishing, like life, is full of trial and error. The greatest fishermen embrace mistakes as opportunities for growth, seeking out fresh challenges while using past lessons to refine their craft. It's not about perfection, but about continuous learning and improvement.

"Many of the most highly publicised events of my presidency are not nearly as memorable or significant in my life as fishing with my daddy."

In the end, it's the simple, quiet moments that often hold the greatest value. Fishing with a loved one becomes a timeless memory, one that stays with us far longer than the fleeting demands of success or fame. It's a reminder that true significance is found in connection, not achievement.

"Fishing is unquestionably a form of madness but, happily, for the once-bitten there is no cure."

Fishing invites us into a world where logic takes a back seat to curiosity and wonder. It's not about reason, but about a deeper connection to the moment. Once we've tasted that, the draw is undeniable – and we return not for answers, but for the experience itself.

"The solution to any problem – work, love, money, whatever – is to go fishing, and the worse the problem, the longer the trip should be."

Sometimes, the best way to solve life's most tangled problems is to step away from them entirely. Fishing offers the perfect escape – a space to clear the mind, gain perspective, and return refreshed. The deeper the challenge, the greater the need for quiet reflection, away from the noise.

"I love fishing. You put that line in the water and you don't know what's on the other end. Your imagination is under there."

Fishing taps into the thrill of the unknown. Each cast is an invitation to dream, to wonder what lies beneath the surface, unseen and full of potential. It's not just about what you catch, but about the endless possibilities that fuel the imagination with every cast.

Paul Schullery

"To fish is to hold a mirror to nature."

Fishing offers a chance to reflect – not just on the world around us, but on ourselves. It's a quiet observation of nature's rhythms, where the line between us and the wild becomes blurred. In these moments, we see not just the water, but our place within it.

"Fishing brings out the reverence of the harmony of all things."

In the stillness of fishing, we come to appreciate the quiet symphony of life. The water, the air, the rhythm of the cast – they all work together in perfect balance. Fishing reminds us of the interconnectedness of everything, where every moment holds the beauty of a greater harmony.

"Rivers and the inhabitants of the watery elements are made for wise men to contemplate and for fools to pass by without consideration."

The quiet flow of rivers holds lessons for those willing to listen. While some rush past, missing the deeper truths in nature's subtle rhythms, others find wisdom in the stillness. Fishing teaches us to slow down and pay attention to what others often overlook – the quiet messages hidden beneath the surface.

"Somebody just back of you while you are fishing is as bad as someone looking over your shoulder while you write a letter to your girl."

Fishing, like any personal moment of reflection, demands solitude. The presence of others can disrupt the flow, much like an intruder on our most intimate thoughts. It's in these quiet, uninterrupted moments that we connect most deeply – with both nature and ourselves.

"A man may fish with the worm that hath eat of a king, and eat of the fish that hath fed of that worm."

Life's cycles are endlessly intertwined. From the smallest creatures to the grandest, we're all part of a larger chain. In fishing, we see this connection clearly – every catch holds a story, tracing back to something much larger than itself, reminding us of our place within the endless flow of nature.

"Again, the Kingdom of Heaven is like a dragnet, that was cast into the sea, and gathered some fish of every kind, which, when it was filled, they drew up on the beach. They sat down and gathered the good into containers, but the bad they threw away."

In fishing, as in life, we are presented with a multitude of opportunities. The dragnet pulls in all things, yet it's in the discerning choice – separating what serves us from what doesn't – that we find clarity. Just as fishermen sort their catch, we too must carefully decide what we hold on to and what we let go.

"He who wants to catch fish must not mind getting wet."

Success often requires discomfort. Whether it's getting your hands dirty or stepping out of your comfort zone, the rewards are reserved for those willing to embrace the challenge. Fishing teaches us that growth and achievement aren't always neat or easy – but they're always worth it.

"Do not tell fish stories where the people know you. Particularly, don't tell them where they know the fish."

The value of a story lies in its mystery. When we share too much, we risk losing the magic that makes it special. Like a fisherman who keeps his best spots secret, sometimes the stories we tell are more powerful when we leave a little something to the imagination.

052

John D. Voelker

"Fly-fishing is a magic way to recapture the rapture of solitude without the pangs of loneliness."

Solitude can be both a sanctuary and a challenge. Fly-fishing offers a unique balance – it invites stillness while connecting us to nature, filling the quiet with purpose rather than emptiness. In these moments, we find peace without isolation, a true retreat for both the mind and the spirit.

053

John Gierach

"Fly-fishing is solitary, contemplative, misanthropic, scientific in some hands, poetic in others, and laced with conflicting aesthetic considerations. It's not even clear if catching fish is actually the point."

Fly fishing is an art that transcends mere sport. It's a fusion of science, philosophy, and poetry, where the act of fishing becomes a personal exploration. The pursuit itself – the quiet focus, the rhythm, the dance with nature – is as valuable as any catch, offering a deeper connection to the world than the fish ever could.

"It has always been my private conviction that any man who pits his intelligence against a fish and loses has it coming."

Fishing challenges us to think, adapt, and outwit nature. But in the end, the fish always have the upper hand in their own domain. It's a reminder that humility is key – no matter how clever we think we are, there are forces in nature that remind us of our place.

"It is impossible to grow weary of a sport that is never the same on any two days of the year."

Fishing stays fresh because nature never repeats itself. The light, the water, the mood of the fish: they all change, making each outing feel like the first.

"It is my great hope that we all come to see the ocean, not as a dark and distant place with little relevance to our lives on land, but as the lifeblood of our home."

The ocean is not separate from our lives; it's the very foundation of them. Understanding its importance means recognising that its well-being directly impacts ours.

"When you fish for love, bait with your heart, not your brain."

Love, like fishing, calls for sincerity. Cleverness may catch attention, but only honesty lands something real. The strongest bonds begin when you cast out with feeling, not strategy.

"The good fisherman is always engaged in the active exercise of his imagination. He is the fish he catches."

Fishing blurs the line between hunter and hunted. To succeed, you must think like the fish – anticipate, imagine, adapt. It's less about domination, more about empathy in motion.

D. C. Reid

"When I fish,
the boundary between
nature and me
disappears. I am
simply another part
of it, not a man isolated
from his source."

Fishing dissolves the illusion of separation. In that stillness,
we stop observing nature and start becoming it.

"Angling is extremely time-consuming. That's sort of the whole point."

Angling isn't about quick results; it's about embracing the time spent.
In the stillness, the experience becomes the true catch.

"Govern a great nation as you would cook a small fish. Do not overdo it."

True mastery, whether in leadership or fishing, lies in restraint. It's about knowing when to step back and let things evolve on their own, without overcomplicating or overworking the process.

"When you are on the river, ocean or in the woods, you are the closest to the truth you'll ever get."

The peace of nature has a way of cutting through life's noise. In the quiet moments by the water, we're reminded of what truly matters.

John Ashley-Cooper

"One thing becomes clearer as one gets older and one's fishing experience increases, and that is the paramount importance of one's fishing companions."

Fishing is more than just a solitary pursuit; it's about shared moments and learning from others. As you grow in skill and experience, the people you fish with become just as important as the fish themselves.

"All streams flow into the sea, yet the sea is never full. To the place the streams come from, there they return again."

Everything in life is interconnected and constantly in motion, with no true end or finality. We are all part of a larger, continuous flow, where what we give or experience eventually returns to its origin.

"The angling fever is a very real disease and can only be cured by the application of cold water and fresh, untainted air."

Angling isn't just a pastime; it's an obsession that pulls you in, making you crave the simplicity of nature. The remedy isn't in escaping the pull, but in fully immersing yourself in the environment, allowing the water and fresh air to reset your mind and soul.

"There is certainly something in angling that tends to produce a gentleness of spirit and a pure sincerity of mind."

Angling slows you down and quiets your thoughts, drawing you into a space where reflection and patience take precedence. It fosters a calm mind, free of distractions, and brings clarity that often eludes us in the rush of daily life.

Charles Kuralt

"Often I have been exhausted on trout streams, uncomfortable, wet, cold, briar scarred, sunburned, mosquito bitten, but never, with a fly rod in my hand, have I been in a place that was less than beautiful."

The journey, despite its discomforts, transforms the experience into something profound. Even in challenging conditions, the pursuit of fishing connects us to beauty in unexpected ways, reminding us that value is found not just in the destination but in the effort and surroundings themselves.

"Never leave fish to find fish."

Focus on the task at hand. The pursuit of something better can distract you from the opportunities right in front of you. By staying present, you increase your chances of success.

"Half the charm
of fishing is that
it generally takes
one into beautiful
scenery. Catching
fish is not all
of fishing."

Fishing is as much about the experience as it is about the catch.
The surroundings, the stillness, and the connection with nature
are just as important as the outcome. It's a chance to escape and
appreciate beauty in its quietest forms.

"The secret of successful fishing is to expect it… Hope should be in the fisherman's heart, expectancy in his hand, and his motto should be 'you can never tell'."

The secret to success in fishing lies in cultivating a mindset of hopeful expectation. It's not about waiting passively, but rather actively believing that success is possible, even if it's uncertain.

"The man who hurries through a Trout stream defeats himself. Not only does he take few fish, but he has no time for observation, and his experience is likely to be of little value to him."

Rushing to the goal leads to mistakes and missed opportunities. The real success lies in taking your time to observe and learn along the way – speed doesn't bring insight, careful attention does.

"There is no greater fan of fly fishing than the worm."

Sometimes, the most elegant solutions come from stepping away from the obvious path. Just as fly fishing doesn't rely on the common worm, finding success in life often means not following the tried-and-tested methods, but instead embracing a more creative or unconventional approach.

"There is time to go long, time to go short and time to go fishing."

Knowing when to act and when to step back is an art. Just as there are moments for big risks and others for precision, the same holds for taking time to pause and recharge. Sometimes, the most valuable decision is to step away from the hustle and allow space for clarity and reflection.

"Fishing is the opposite of war."

Fishing invites you to step away from the chaos of conflict and find a space where focus and stillness replace urgency and combat. It's a reminder that some solutions come not through force, but through careful observation and a calm approach.

"Fishing is still elemental in the most elemental sense of the word – an activity composed of water and air and light and space, all arranged in precarious balance around a central idea of a man in a boat, waiting for a bite."

Amid the complexity of modern life, fishing returns us to the purest elements, reminding us that the deepest experiences often come from the simplest ingredients, perfectly aligned.

"A big fish is caught with big bait."

Big challenges often require bold actions. Just as a large fish is attracted to a sizeable bait, our most significant achievements come when we're willing to take risks and step out of our comfort zones. It's a reminder that in order to reel in something truly remarkable, we must be prepared to cast our nets wide and put in the effort that matches our aspirations.

"I've gone fishing thousands of times in my life, and I have never once felt unlucky or poorly paid for those hours on the water."

Some pursuits are measured not by outcomes, but by the peace they bring. To fish is to be paid in quiet moments, shifting light, and the gentle passing of time – riches that never lose their value.

"After living for nearly 100 years on this planet, I now understand the most important place on Earth is not on land, but at sea."

The sea is where life begins and thrives, far beyond the land we inhabit. It reminds us that the most important parts of our world are not always the ones we can control, but those we rely on silently, without thought.

"The fish caught in the net starts to think."

Fishing teaches us the value of hindsight – how only when we're no longer in control our choices become clearer. It's a reminder to reflect on our actions before we find ourselves caught.

"The sea is only the embodiment of a supernatural and wonderful existence. It is nothing but love and emotion; it is the Living Infinite."

The sea embodies an endless source of wonder, where each wave tells a story of renewal and infinity. It's a reminder that life is not just about what we see, but the deep currents of emotion and potential that lie beneath.

"Fishes live in the sea, as men do on land: the great ones eat up the little ones."

In life, power dynamics often play out in ways we don't always recognise. The larger forces tend to consume the smaller, but the real challenge lies in how we navigate, adapt, and find our place within these currents.

"The opposite
of courage is not
cowardice, it is
conformity. Even
a dead fish can
go with the flow."

True courage isn't about avoiding fear. It's about resisting the pull of mediocrity and standing up for what's right, even if it means swimming against the current.

Arthur C. Clarke

"How inappropriate to call this planet Earth when it is quite clearly Ocean."

The planet's true essence lies beneath the surface, where the ocean dominates, reminding us that the Earth's identity is shaped more by the vast waters than by the land we inhabit.

"The sea has neither meaning nor pity."

The sea exists beyond human concerns, offering no explanations or compassion, reflecting nature's indifference to our desires and struggles.

Barry López

"To put your hands in a river is to feel the chords that bind the Earth together."

The river represents the interconnectedness of life, where every drop contributes to the larger, unseen force that unites all things on Earth.

"If you cannot catch a fish, do not blame the sea."

When things don't go as planned, it's easy to point fingers. But often, the issue lies not with the circumstances but with how we approach them. Success in any endeavour requires patience, adaptability, and understanding – qualities we can control.

"Anyone can be a fisherman in May."

The ease of success can often be deceptive. When conditions are perfect, anyone can succeed. True skill and resilience show when the circumstances aren't ideal, and perseverance becomes more important than luck.

"Fishing is not so much getting fish as it is a state of mind."

Fishing creates a quiet space where time slows down and the noise fades. It's less about the catch and more about the clarity that comes when you simply allow yourself to be.

"You must lose a fly to catch a trout."

To gain what you seek, you may have to let go of something along the way. It's about understanding that progress often involves giving up something in the short term for a larger reward.

"Perhaps I should not have been a fisherman, he thought. But that was the thing that I was born for."

The journey of self-discovery is often rooted in realising what feels instinctively right, even when doubt creeps in. It's not about making the right choice – it's about embracing what calls you.

Lao Tzu

"The river moves effortlessly, reminding us of the path of least resistance."

The river teaches us that sometimes the simplest path is the most effective. By allowing life to flow naturally and without force, we can navigate challenges with grace. Resistance only makes the journey harder – wisdom lies in moving with the current, not against it.

"To go fishing is discipline in the equality of men – for all men are equal before fish."

Nature doesn't discriminate. Fishing strips away titles and statuses, reminding us of our shared humanity and the simple truths that unite us.

"The fish you release may be a gift to another, as it may have been a gift to you."

Releasing a fish isn't just an act of letting go; it's passing on an opportunity for someone else to experience the same thrill. What we give today can return in unexpected ways, creating a cycle of shared moments and unseen connections.

"We are tied to the ocean. And when we go back to the sea, whether it is to sail or to watch – we are going back from whence we came."

The sea is a reminder of our roots, an eternal connection that calls us back to our beginnings, grounding us in a place where we feel both lost and found at the same time.

"A wise fisherman always casts his net on both sides of the boat."

Wisdom often lies in expanding our perspective. By casting a wide net – exploring different angles and considering all possibilities – we increase our chances of success. In fishing, as in life, balance and openness lead to greater opportunities.

Acknowledgements

To my late grandpa Mossie, who was the strongest example of what it means to be noble, moral, and a great man. Your encouraging 'words of wisdom' shaped me and inspired this entire series. I think of you always and strive to live up to the remarkable example you set for all who knew you.

To my parents, Robert and Joanne, and my brothers, Liam and Wyatt, thank you for nurturing my curiosity, encouraging my creativity, and always offering honest, thoughtful feedback. Each of you, as creatives in your own right, has played a key role in shaping my ideas, and I am fortunate to have your support and perspective. *Fishing*, as the first book in this series, holds a special significance. It's rooted in early memories of time spent by the water with my brothers – moments that quietly influenced the way I see the world.

To Vladislava, who supported this project from the very beginning. Thank you for sharing in every moment of joy along the way – and for ordering the very first copy before I even realised it was out.

I'd also like to extend my heartfelt thanks to Marc, my publisher, for believing in this project and taking a leap of faith to work with me on my very first book. Our first in-person meeting over coffee at the London Design Museum – exploring their beautiful collection of books and talking all things *Worlds of Wisdom* – set the stage for something truly exciting. I hope there are many more to follow.

The quotes and sayings in *Worlds of Wisdom – Fishing* are shared in the spirit of reflection and the pursuit of timeless insight. While every effort has been made to credit original sources, some are difficult to trace due to their historical and cultural origins. This book is not intended as a scholarly reference, but as a curated collection of meaningful words – thoughtfully selected, interpreted, and beautifully presented. Corrections are welcomed for future editions.

References

001 Hoover, H. (1963) *Fishing for Fun – and to Wash Your Soul*. New York: Random House.

002 Heraclitus (c.500 BC) Fragments. In: Freeman, K. (trans.) (1949) *Ancilla to the Pre-Socratic Philosophers*. Cambridge, MA: Harvard University Press.

003 Larson, D. (n.d.) 'If people concentrated on the really important things in life, there'd be a shortage of fishing poles.' Available at: *www.brainyquote.com/quotes/doug_larson_107974* (Accessed: 15 May 2025).

004 Shedd, J.A. (1928) *Salt from My Attic*. Portland, ME: The Mosher Press.

005 Unknown (n.d.) 'When fishermen cannot go to sea, they repair nets.' Available at: *www.goodreads.com/quotes/8790564-when-fishermen-cannot-go-to-sea-they-repair-nets* (Accessed: 15 May 2025).

006 Cousteau, J.-Y. (1971) *Life and Death in a Coral Sea*. Garden City, NY: Doubleday.

007 Thoreau, H.D. (1853) Journal Entry: January 26, 1853. In: Torrey, B. and Allen, F.H. (eds.) (1906) *The Journal of Henry D. Thoreau*. Boston: Houghton Mifflin.

008 Unknown (n.d.) 'It's called fishing, not catching.' Available at: *theactivistangler.org/itscalled-fishing-not-catching* (Accessed: 15 May 2025).

009 Middleton, H. (1989) *The Earth Is Enough: Growing Up in a World of Flyfishing, Trout & Old Men*. New York: Simon & Schuster.

010 Dinesen, I. (1934) *Seven Gothic Tales*. New York: Harrison Smith and Robert Haas.

011 Twain, M. (1883) *Life on the Mississippi*. Boston: James R. Osgood & Company. Paraphrased from Chapter 9.

012 Safina, C. (2011) *The View from Lazy Point: A Natural Year in an Unnatural World*. New York: Henry Holt and Company.

013 van Gogh, V. (1882) Letter to Theo van Gogh, 14 May. Available at: *www.webexhibits.org/vangogh/letter/11/193.htm* (Accessed: 15 May 2025).

014 Attenborough, D. (2025) *Ocean with David Attenborough* [Documentary film]. Silverback Films & Open Planet Studios.

015 Traver, R. (1964) *Trout Madness*. New York: Holt, Rinehart and Winston.

016 Houston, J. (2012) *Catch of the Day: Spiritual Lessons for Life from the Sport of Fishing*. Nashville: Thomas Nelson. Paraphrase reflecting Houston's view on the evolving nature of fishing.

017 Blake, T. (n.d.) 'Some go to church to think about fishing, others go fishing to think about God.' Jackson Community Church Reflections. Available at: *www.southernliving.com/culture/fishing-quotes* (Accessed: 15 May 2025)

018 Watkins, J.N. (n.d.) 'A river cuts through rock, not because of its power, but because of its persistence.' Available at: *barrypopik.com/blog/strength_a_river_cuts_through_a_rock* (Accessed: 12 June 2025)

019 Cousteau, J.-Y. (n.d.) 'The sea, the great unifier, is man's only hope. Now, as never before, the old phrase has a literal meaning: we are all in the same boat.' AZQuotes. Available at: *www.azquotes.com/quote/66083* (Accessed: 12 June 2025)

020 Ray, J. (1670) *A Complete Collection of English Proverbs*. (Reprint edn., 1813) London: John Belfour.

021 da Vinci, L. (1906) *Thoughts on Art and Life*. Edited by Maurice Baring. London: Dent.

022 Haig-Brown, R. (1946) *A River Never Sleeps*. Toronto: McClelland & Stewart [paraphrase]. Inspiring statement attributed to Haig-Brown, based on his writings.

023 Conrad, J. (1906) *The Mirror of the Sea*. London: J. M. Dent, Chapter 35.

024 Haig-Brown, R.L. (1946) *A River Never Sleeps*. Toronto: McClelland & Stewart.

025 Cousteau, J.-Y. (n.d.) 'We forget that the water cycle and the life cycle are one.'

All-Creatures Quotations Archive. Available at: *www.all-creatures.org/quotes/costeau-jacques. html* (Accessed: 12 June 2025).

026 Haig-Brown, R.L. (1946) *A River Never Sleeps*. Toronto: McClelland & Stewart. Paraphrase based on Haig-Brown's reflections on listening to rivers.

027 Walton, I. (1653) *The Compleat Angler*. London: Richard Marriot. Paraphrased interpretation.

028 Emerson, R.W. (1870) *Society and Solitude*. United States: Fields, Osgood, & Co. Paraphrased interpretation.

029 Gordon, T. (1947) *The Complete Fly Fisherman: The Notes and Letters of Theodore Gordon*. New York: Scribners.

030 Gierach, J. (1994) *Dances with Trout*. New York: Simon & Schuster. Paraphrase of thematic idea.

031 Haig-Brown, R.L. (1946) *A River Never Sleeps*. Toronto: McClelland & Stewart.

032 Korean Proverb (n.d.) 'Even a fish wouldn't get into trouble if it kept its mouth shut'. Available at: *www.worldofproverbs.com/2012/03/even-fish-wouldnt-get-into-trouble-if.html* (Accessed: 12 June 2025)

033 Lao Tzu (c.6th century BC) *Tao Te Ching*. Paraphrase reflecting Lao Tzu's views on contentment and simplicity. This is a modern, but popular paraphrase.

034 Hughes, T. (n.d.) 'Fishing provides that connection with the whole living world…' Quoted in analysis of the poem Pike. Available at: *www.goodreads.com/quotes/780968-fishingprovides-that-connection-with-the-whole-living-world-it* (Accessed: 12 June 2025).

035 German Proverb (n.d.) 'It is good fishing in troubled waters.' In: Christy, R. (1887) *Proverbs, Maxims and Phrases of All Ages*. London.

036 Walton, I. (1653) *The Compleat Angler*. London: Richard Marriot. Epistle to the Reader.

037 Waterman, C.W. (n.d.) 'Most of the world is covered by water. A fisherman's job is simple: Pick out the best parts.' Quoted in AZQuotes. Available at: *www.azquotes.com/quote/1751202* (Accessed: 12 June 2025).

038 Wetherell, W.D., (1998). *Vermont River*. Hanover: University Press of New England.

039 Gierach, J., (2000). *Standing in a River Waving a Stick*. New York: Simon & Schuster.

040 Carter, J., (1994). *An Outdoor Journal: Adventures and Reflections*. Fayetteville: University of Arkansas Press.

041 Home, A. V. G., (1976). *The Way the Wind Blows*. London: William Heinemann.

042 Gierach, J., (2000). *Standing in a River Waving a Stick*. New York: Simon & Schuster.

043 Altman, R., (2004). 'Robert Altman: What I've Learned.' *Esquire*, 1 February. Available at: *classic.esquire.com/article/2004/2/1/what-ive-learned-robert-altman* (Accessed: 12 June 2025).

044 Schullery, P., (2013). *The Fishing Life: An Angler's Tales of Wild Rivers and Other Restless Metaphors*. New York: Skyhorse Publishing.

045 Trueblood, T. (n.d.) 'Fishing brings out the reverence of the harmony of all things.' Paraphrase based on Trueblood's philosophy in *Field & Stream* magazine writings.

046 Walton, I. (1653; ed. 1859) *The Compleat Angler*, Part I, Chapter 1. London: Routledge and Co.

047 Hemingway, E. (2012) *Hemingway on Fishing*, ed. N.Lyons and J. Hemingway. New York: Simon & Schuster.

048 Shakespeare, W. (1653/1859) *Hamlet*, Act 4, Scene 3. London: Routledge.

049 *The Holy Bible*: King James Version (2000) London: Collins.

050 Spanish Proverb (n.d.) 'He who wants to catch fish must not mind getting wet.' [Proverb]

051 Twain, M. (1927) More Maxims of Mark. In: Johnson, M.D. (comp.) *Mark Twain at Your Fingertips: A Book of Quotations*. New York: Courier Corporation.

052 Voelker, J.D. (n.d.) Fly-fishing is a magic way to recapture the rapture of solitude without the pangs of loneliness. Quoted in AZQuotes. Available at: *www.azquotes.com/quote/1126664* (Accessed: 12 June 2025).

053 Gierach, J. (1994) *Dances with Trout*. New York: Simon & Schuster.

054 Steinbeck, J. (1954) 'It has always been my private conviction that any man who pits his intelligence against a fish and loses has it coming.' *Punch*, 25 August.

055 Gordon, T. (1909) *The Complete Fly Fisherman*. New York: Forest and Stream Publishing Company.

056 Attenborough, D. (2025) *Ocean with David Attenborough* [Documentary film]. Silverback Films & Open Planet Studios.

057 Twain, M. (1898) Notebook [unpublished manuscript]. Quoted in *Mark Twain at Your Fingertips: A Book of Quotations*. New York: Courier Corporation.

058 Paxman, J. (1995) *Fish, Fishing and the Meaning of Life*. London: Penguin.

059 Reid, D. C. (2005) *Fishing for Dreams: Notes from the Water's Edge*. Victoria, BC: Mother Tongue Publishing.

060 McGuane, T. (2000) *The Longest Silence: A Life in Fishing*. New York: Atlantic Monthly Press.

061 Lao Tzu (1963) *Tao Te Ching*, trans. D.C. Lau. Harmondsworth: Penguin Books.

062 Leonard, J. (n.d.) 'When you are on the river, ocean or in the woods, you are the closest to the truth you'll ever get.' [Attributed, unverified].

063 Ashley-Cooper, J. (1975) *The Complete Angler*. London: Hamlyn.

064 *Holy Bible* (1611), King James Version. London: Robert Barker. Ecclesiastes 1:7.

065 Gordon, T. (1909) *Notes on Trout Fishing*. New York: Houghton Mifflin.

066 Irving, W. (1860) *The Sketch Book of Geoffrey Crayon, Gent*. New York: G.P. Putnam.

067 Kuralt, C. (1977) *A Life on the Road*. New York: Random House.

068 Proverb. (n.d.) Traditional saying attributed to Moses.

069 Hutton, J.A. (1912) *Fishing*. London: Methuen & Co.

070 Hartman, R. (1935) *About Fishing*. London: Arthur Barker Ltd.

071 La Branche, G. M. L. (1914) *The Dry Fly and Fast Water: Fishing with the Floating Fly on American Trout Streams*. New York: Charles Scribner's Sons.

072 McManus, P.F. (1984) *Never Sniff a Gift Fish*. New York: Macmillan.

073 Livermore, J. L. (1940) *How to Trade in Stocks: The Livermore Formula for Combining Time Element and Price*. New York: Duell, Sloan & Pearce.

074 Orwell, G. (1946) *Inside the Whale and Other Essays*. London: Victor Gollancz.

075 Subramanian, S. (2012) *Following Fish: Travels Around the Indian Coast*. London: Atlantic Books.

076 African proverb (n.d.) 'A big fish is caught with big bait.' Available at: *www.reelcoquina fishing.com/blogs/florida-fishing-blog/best-fishing-quotes* (Accessed: 12 June 2025).

077 Tapply, W.G. (1994) *A Beginner's Guide to Fishing*. New York: Simon & Schuster.

078 Attenborough, D. (2025) *Ocean with David Attenborough* [Documentary film]. Silverback Films & Open Planet Studios.

079 Zanzibar Proverb (n.d.) 'The fish caught in the net starts to think.' [Proverb].

080 Verne, J. (1870) *Twenty Thousand Leagues Under the Sea*. Translated by W.H.G. Kingston. London: Sampson Low, Marston, Searle, & Rivington.

081 Shakespeare, W. (1609) The Merchant of Venice. In: *The Complete Works of William Shakespeare*. Edited by W.J. Craig. London: Oxford University Press, 1914, act 1, scene 3.

082 Hightower, J. (2004) *Thieves in High Places: They've Stolen Our Country and It's Time to Take It Back*. New York: Penguin.

083 Clarke, A. C. (n.d.) 'How inappropriate to call this planet Earth when it is clearly Ocean.' [Quote]. Available at: *www.goodreads.com/quotes/109398-how-inappropriate-to-call-this-planetearth-when-it-is* (Accessed: 12 June 2025).

084 Chekhov, A. (1890) 'Gusev', in *Chekhov: The Complete Short Stories*. Translated by Constance Garnett. London: Vintage Classics, 1998.

085 Lopez, B., (1990). *River Notes: The Dance of Herons*. London: Picador.

086 Greek proverb (n.d.) 'If you cannot catch a fish, do not blame the sea.' [Proverb].

087 Hemingway, E., (1952). *The Old Man and the Sea*. New York: Charles Scribner's Sons.

088 Flick, A., (1974). *Art Flick's New Streamside Guide to Naturals and Their Imitations*. New York: Winchester Press.

089 Herbert, G., (1651). *Jacula Prudentum: A Golden Treasury of the Best Thoughts of the Best Thinkers*. London: Humphrey Moseley.

090 Hemingway, E., (1952). *The Old Man and the Sea*. New York: Charles Scribner's Sons.

091 Lao Tzu (c.6th century BC) *Tao Te Ching*. Paraphrased interpretation inspired by Taoist or Zen philosophy, especially ideas found in the *Tao Te Ching*.

092 Hoover, H. (1963) *Fishing for Fun – and to Wash Your Soul*. New York: Random House.

093 Wulff, L. (1964) *Handbook of Freshwater Fishing*. New York: Knopf.

094 Kennedy, J.F. (1962) 'Remarks in Newport at the Australian Ambassador's Dinner for the America's Cup Crews', 14 September 1962. Public Papers of the Presidents: John F. Kennedy, 1962. Available at: *www.jfklibrary.org/learn/about-jfk/life-of-john-f-kennedy/john-f-kennedy-quotations* (Accessed: 12 June 2025).

095 African Proverb (n.d.) 'A wise fisherman always casts his net on both sides of the boat.' [Proverb]

Worlds of Wisdom
FISHING
The Art of Living, One Insight at a Time

Concept, research and writing
Asher Erskine

Text editing
Sandy Logan

Illustrations
Asher Erskine

Graphic design
Sarah Schrauwen & Mathieu Vancamp,
doublebill.design

D/2025/12.005/12
ISBN 9789460583872
NUR 450

© 2025 Luster Publishing, Antwerp
info@lusterpublishing.com
lusterpublishing.com
@lusterbooks

Subscribe to our newsletter for new book
alerts and a look behind the scenes:

About the author

Asher Erskine is a multidisciplinary
designer from London and Head of
Design at E1 Series. With a background
spanning industrial design, architecture,
interiors, fashion, and branding,
he also speaks internationally on
design and innovation.

Raised in a home shaped by art,
imagination, and invention, Asher
grew up immersed in craftsmanship
and storytelling. Inspired by his
late grandfather Mossie's 'words of
wisdom', he developed a deep respect
for the power of ideas and the wisdom
passed down through generations.